WRITE YOUR OWN FAIRY TALE

a workbook of activities to guide you to your own fairy tale

by Alyssa Curtayne

All content is compiled and created by Alyssa Curtayne. Alyssa Curtayne, trading as Rising Spirit; Where Great Ideas Grow, retains the worldwide copyright of this product and the accompanying online course.
All content ©Alyssa Curtayne 2023

Welcome to Write Your Own Fairy Tale

In this course, it is our goal to help you do three things:
1. Understand the basic structure of fairy tales
2. Tap into your own intuition to find your story
3. Have a finished product you can then keep, share or publish

Fairy tales have longevity, because they share universal truths about the human condition. Many fairy tales have elements of real people in magical circumstances. Fairy tales date back to global mythology and the oral tradition of story-sharing. Each new generation changes and redefines them. But there's no reason we can't create our own fairy tales about ourselves for today. Enjoy!

My definition of fairy tales

My favourite fairy tales

The most common fairy tales

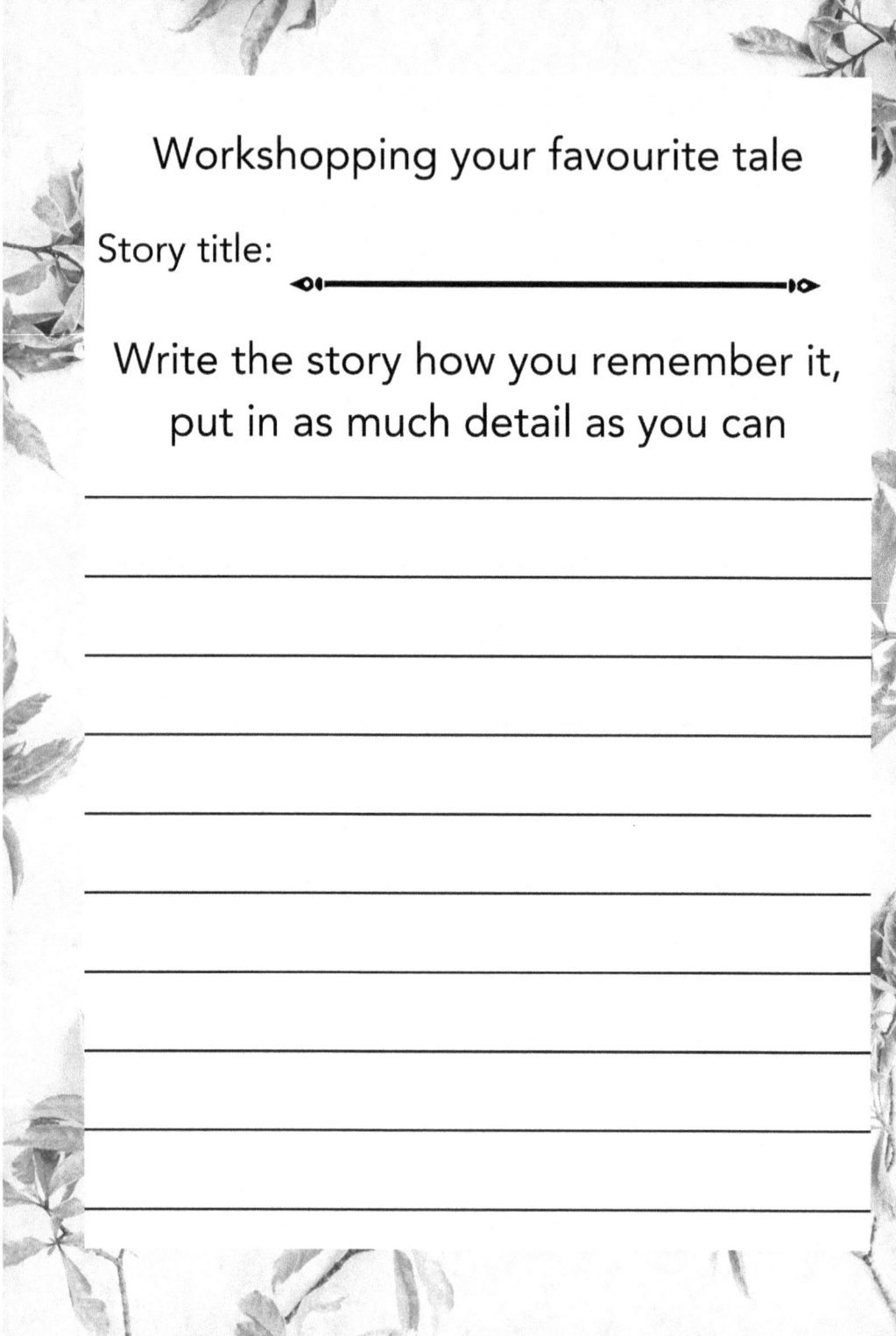

Write the story in seven sentences

Summarise in three sentences

Summarise in one line

Why I like this fairy tale

How it connects with my life today

___
___
___
___
___
___
___
___

Themes (main ideas)

What this story taught me about life

Brainstorm the general features of fairy tales

Free writing activity - select one item from your brainstorm and write freely about that topic.

Write your fairy tale into this simple structure

Once upon a time (setting, character)
_____
_____

Suddenly, (something happened) _____
_____
_____

And then _____
_____

And then _____
_____

And then _____
_____

Until _____
_____

So then _____
_____

What aspect of this story do you resonate with the most? Is it a feeling? Colour? Setting? Character? Scene?

Authenticity - when do you remember feeling your authentic self?

My list of what makes me, me

On the next page we have an activity called "Significant Moments". The idea of this activity is for you to think of 3-5 significant moments in your life - births, deaths, celebrations, disappointments, or other significant moments of your life. You can either write a few words or draw a simple image that represents your moment. There are no incorrect answers here.

If you need mental support, reach out to your mental health professional.

Significant moments

Pick ONE significant moment and write in this format:

Once upon a time (setting, character) _____
_____
_____

Suddenly, (something happened) _____
_____
_____

And then _____
_____

And then _____
_____

And then _____
_____

Until _____
_____

So then _____
_____

What do you notice in your story when you compare it to your fairy tale?

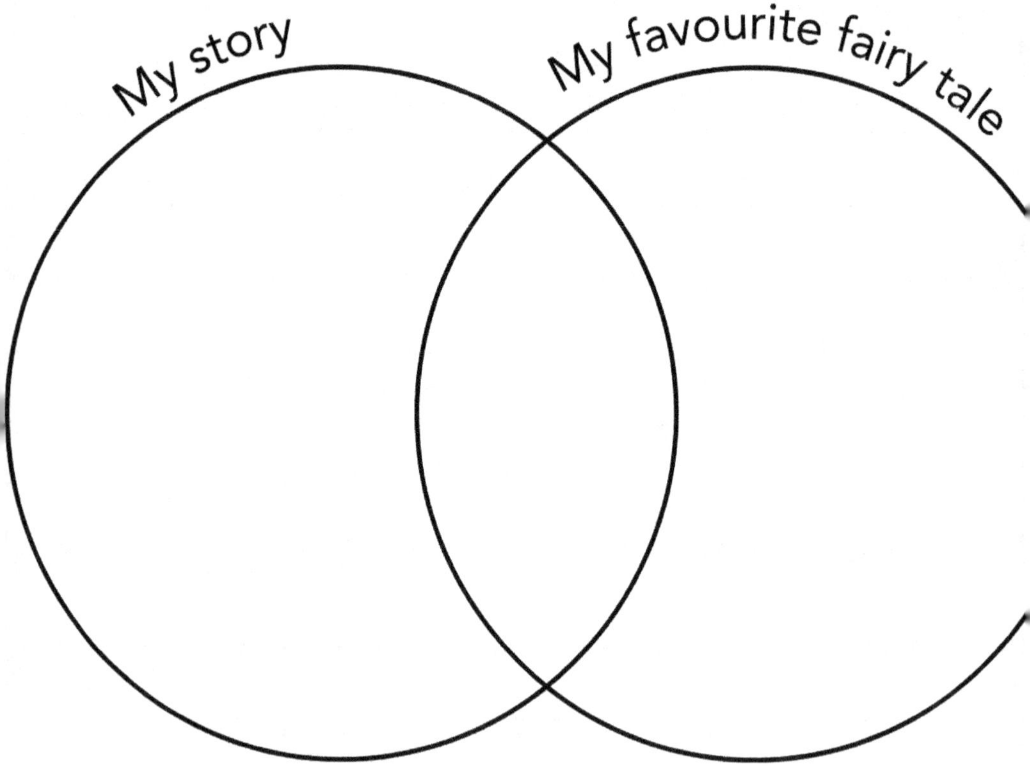

My story

My favourite fairy tale

Workshopping your story - rewrite and expand your simple structured story

_____

_____

_____

_____

_____

_____

_____

_____

_____

_____

Consider the following in your edits and re-writes. Have fun with it:

- shifting point of view of the main character to another character
- characters - do you have too many? not enough? Do they capture an archetypal model?
- plot repetition - 3, 5, 7 - will it strengthen your story?
- themes - are they clear?
- setting - is it a traditional fairy tale setting or a modern one? Have you set it in a fantasy world? real-world?
- symbolism - what symbols/motifs can you add or include?
- ending - is it fulfilling?
- moral lesson - is it subtle? or explicit? is there one?
- spelling and grammatical checks

Editing

Change the point of view to a secondary character

Setting

Try your story in different settings

Symbolism

What symbols or motifs could you add to make it a stronger story?

___
___
___
___
___
___
___
___
___
___

Rewrite your draft including some of the new ideas

What next?

Congratulations! You have finished a draft of your very own fairy tale. So what next? You can rest the story for a few months before coming back to edit, you can give it to a writing buddy or editor to check and offer suggestions or you may want to enter it into writing competitions.

You may want to go back to the start and do another fairy tale and another significant moment. The choices are infinite!

There are also communities of people who love fairy tales online and in person whom you might wish to connect with. Either way, keep writing!

About the author:
Alyssa has been teaching for 30+ years. She has a Graduate Certificate in Creative Writing from Deakin University, is a member of the Australian Fairy Tale Society, an oral storyteller (specialising in folk and fairy tales) is a former journalist and sub-editor, a former English teacher and a lover of the ability of stories to transform and transport us into our shared humanity. You can follow her at alyssacurtaynestories

www.ingramcontent.com/pod-product-compliance
Lightning Source LLC
Chambersburg PA
CBHW070714020526
44107CB00078B/2575